The Rajah
of Chutneypore

The Rajah
of Chutneypore

George Dance and
Frank Desprez

MINT EDITIONS

The Rajah of Chutneypore was first published in 1891.

This edition published by Mint Editions 2021.

ISBN 9781513281377 | E-ISBN 9781513286396

Published by Mint Editions®

MINT
EDITIONS

minteditionbooks.com

Publishing Director: Jennifer Newens
Design & Production: Rachel Lopez Metzger
Project Manager: Micaela Clark
Typesetting: Westchester Publishing Services

Dramatis Personæ

Punka (the Rajah of Chutneypore)
Indru (his Son)
Pyjama (the Grand Vizier)
Punka's Poor Relations:
    Chinna Loofa
    Suttee
    Cheetah
Baboo Currie (Proprietor of a Nautch Troupe)
Nautch Girls:
    Hollee Beebee
    Banyan
    Kalee
    Tiffin
Bumbo (an Idol)

Nautch Girls, Ladies of the Court, Soldiers, Priests, Coolies, etc.

Act I
A Street in the Outskirts of Chutneypore.

Act II
Courtyard of the Rajah's Palace.

Act I

A street in the outskirts of Chutneypore, Sudras discovered.

OPENING CHORUS.

Beneath the sky of blue
The indolent Hindu
    Reclines the whole day long.
He scorns all worldly trouble,
For life's a fragile bubble,
    And death a sweet, sweet song.
He scorns ambitious schemes,
He weaves no lofty dreams,
    His glance is on the ground.
Why tinge to-day with sorrow
When with the dark to-morrow
    Grim Siva's call may sound?

Enter Indru.

RECITATIVE. INDRU.

This is the place, the sweet and hallowed spot,
And these the folks who share her humble lot.

SUDRAS (*salaaming*): Salaam, Sahib! Salaam, Sahib!

ARIA. INDRU.

Bow not, good people, to the earth,
We all are men of equal worth;
For though a Brahmin such as I
By Hindu law may not come nigh
Plebeian fellows such as ye,
    Yet I despise that harsh decree.
CHORUS: Despise that harsh decree!
INDRU: The year, the day, the hour is past
    When men should serve the Despot Caste,

THE RAJAH OF CHUTNEYPORE   7

CHORUS: When men should serve the Despot Caste!
INDRU: So, there's a hand and there's a hand,
     And grasp it firm and true!
  I love you much, for I am such
     A Democrat Hindu.
CHORUS: Yes! there's a hand, etc.
TENORS: These sentiments are Democrat indeed,
BASSES: But who is this that preaches such a creed?
INDRU: I am Indru, the Rajah's only son.
CHORUS: He is Indru, the Rajah's only son.
They fall back salaaming.
INDRU: Nay, shrink not from me. Rank I have eschewed.
  I am your brother from this day henceforth;
  I love a maid, one of your humble Caste,
  'Mongst you she lives, and where she lives, live I;
  You are her friends, and Beebee's friends are mine.
  List! and I'll tell the story of our love.
     List! list!

BALLAD. INDRU.

  The sun was setting, cool the day,
  And, half asleep, I dreaming lay,
  When, through the window from the street,
  There came a voice so clear and sweet.
  'Twas like the surf o'er pebbles tripping
  Or drops of water drip, drip, dripping
     In a crystal stream.
CHORUS: In a crystal stream.
  'Twas not an ordinary voice
     But something like a dream.
CHORUS: 'Twas not an ordinary voice, etc.
INDRU: I rose, and to the casement flew,
  And what a vision met my view!
  A dancing maid, a thing of grace,
  A Nautch girl with an angel's face.
  'Twas like a cherub's calmly sleeping
  Or Venus through her tresses peeping
     At her bashful love.

CHORUS: At her bashful love.

INDRU: 'Twas not an ordinary face,
       But something from above.

CHORUS: 'Twas not an ordinary face, etc.

(*the following verse appears in the vocal score but not the libretto*)

INDRU: I stood transfixed before my Queen,
    Such beauty I had never seen;
    And while I watched her from above,
    My eyes drank in deep draughts of love.
    'Twas such a sweet ecstatic feeling,
    Like perfume o'er the senses stealing,
       Lulling one to sleep,

CHORUS: Lulling one to sleep.

INDRU: 'Twas not an ordinary love,
       But something far more deep.

CHORUS: 'Twas not an ordinary love, etc.

Enter Baboo Currie.

CURRIE: Who sings of love in such flowery accents?

INDRU: Baboo Currie! (*Currie salaams*) Won't you shake hands?

CURRIE: Not with the Rajah's son.

INDRU: Why not?

CURRIE: You know very well it is unlawful for a Brahmin to shake
    hands with a ballet-master.

INDRU: But if I choose to lower myself to your level? I love one of the
    young ladies of your troupe.

CURRIE (*aside*): Another vacancy in my front row. (*Aloud*) A Nautch
    girl is no fit sweetheart for you. You must forget her.

INDRU: Forget her! I cannot. I think of her all day, and dream of her
    all night. Say what you like, she shall be my wife.

CURRIE (*aside*): Oh, shall she? I'm not going to have my troupe broken
    up into eligible marriage lots in this barefaced manner. (*Aloud*)
    Listen to me. This lady is a member of the lowest Caste, while you
    are of the highest, and the Hindu law distinctly says that persons
    of unequal rank may not marry under pain of death. The lady your
    Highness loves is my principal dancer, Hollee Beebee?

INDRU: Yes.

CURRIE: I thought so. Listen; I returned this morning with my
    troupe from a short provincial tour, and was met at the city gate
    by a chuprassie, who handed me a note from your father. He has

heard of your infatuation, and commands me to put a stop to the affair at once, or

INDRU: Or what?

CURRIE: He will cancel my music and dancing license.

INDRU: What steps can you take in the matter?

CURRIE: Well, of a dancing master can't take steps, I should like to know who can. I shall command her to return your presents and letters forthwith.

INDRU: And if she refuse?

CURRIE: I shall fine her a week's salary. You'd better reconsider the matter. She's not the only girl in the world.

INDRU: She's the only girl in my heart.

DUET.—INDRU AND CURRIE.

INDRU: Roses are fair, but not fairer than she.

CURRIE: Of feminine beauty beware, Sir!

INDRU: Rubies are bright, but not brighter to me.

CURRIE: You see her without her back hair, Sir.

INDRU: Sages are wise, but not wiser, I vow.

CURRIE: Her h's she's always misplacing.

INDRU: Cutters are trim, but not trimmer, come now!

CURRIE: The fruits of incessant tight-lacing.

INDRU: But be she plain, what do I care,
　　So long as I believe her fair?
　　　　It's simply a question of taste, you know,

CURRIE: Simply a question of taste.

CHORUS: Simply.

INDRU: This person's gladness
　　　Is that person's sadness,
　　It's simply a question of taste.

CHORUS: It's simply a question of taste.

ALL: You know.

INDRU: Lilies are pure, but not purer than she.

CURRIE: She's more wide-a-wake than you think, Sir,

INDRU: Comrades are true, but not truer to me.

CURRIE: At strangers I've known her to wink, Sir.

INDRU: Willows are lither, but not lither, you'll own.

CURRIE: All thanks to my excellent training.

　　　　　　　GEORGE DANCE AND FRANK DESPREZ

INDRU: Song birds are sweet, but not sweeter in tone.
CURRIE: She can't reach B flat without straining.
INDRU: But be she that, well, what's amiss
    So long as I believe her this?
      It's simply a question of taste, etc.
Exeunt Currie and Chorus.
INDRU: Is there no way by which I can marry Beebee? (*Starting, with a sudden inspiration*) Stay! Could I not renounce my Caste? The thing is simple enough. I have but to eat a little potted cow in public and it is done. Both of the same rank, we may marry, and none can separate us. What is Caste compared with Beebee? I'll do it, and this very day she shall be mine for ever. (*Goes off*)
Enter Banyan, Kalee, Tiffin, and Nautch Girls.

CHORUS.

    With merry song
    We trip along
Threading through the idle throng.
    While from our eyes
    The fire flies
That kindles hope in the unwise.
    We never woo
    As others do
With passion ardent, firm, and true;
    For we would stay
    Unwed for aye,
To love, and love, and run away.
    With merry song, etc.

SOLO. BANYAN.

    The monarch upon his throne
      May hold a mighty sway;
    The sailor upon the sea
      May chant a merry lay;
    The miser amidst his gold
      May chuckle in his pride;
    The maiden upon the quay

May hail the coming tide.
But neither the monarch, nor sailor on sea,
Nor miser with gold, nor maiden on quay,
Are half so contented and happy as we.
CHORUS: Contented and happy as we!
TIFFIN: We call a crust a banquet, and a wail a roundelay,
That's our merry cakes and sherry, hey down derry way!
ALL: We call a crust a banquet, etc.

SOLO. KALEE.

The poet upon a hill
 May dream a blissful dream;
The cattle upon the lea
 May lap the cooling stream;
The children upon the sward
 May skip in mirthful play;
The sparrow upon the tree
 May wake the sleeping day.
But neither the poet, nor cattle on lea,
Nor children on sward, nor sparrow on tree,
Are half so contented and happy as we.
CHORUS: Contented and happy as we!
TIFFIN: We call a cot a palace, and a cloud a golden ray,
That's our merry cakes and sherry, hey down derry way!
ALL: We call a cot a palace, etc.
Enter Beebee.

RECITATIVE. BEEBEE.

And if you ask us whence this endless joy
This happy lot this bliss without alloy?
We answer, 'tis the guerdon of our art,
Which few attain, for few can play the part.

SONG. BEEBEE.

First you take a shapely maiden,
 Tall of stature, sweet of face,

Eyes with hidden mischief laden,
  Limbs that move with lissom grace;
Then you robe this charming creature,
  So her beauty to enhance;
Thus attired, you may teach her
  All the movements of the dance.
    Shape the toe,
    Point it so,
    Hang the head,
    Arms outspread,
    Give the wrist
    Graceful twist,
    Eyes half-closed,
    Now you're posed.
  And the rest is A, B, C;
  Simply one, two, three.
(*the rest of this song appears in the vocal score but not in the libretto*)
BEEBEE (*continuing*): Slowly twirling,
  Creeping, curling,
Swaying like a wind-blown tree;
  Gently stooping,
  Sweeping, drooping,
Slyly counting one, two, three.
CHORUS: A, B, C,
  One, two, three,
  Gently stooping, etc.
BEEBEE: By and bye this shapely maiden
  Will have learned the Nautch girl's art,
And her eyes, with mischief laden,
  Then may play their proper part,
Throwing artful furtive glances
  'Mongst the silent gaping throng,
Wringing heartstrings as she dances,
  Making conquests all along.
    Shape the toe, etc.
CHORUS: A, B, C, etc.
INDRU (*advancing*): Beebee!
BEEBEE (*runs to him he puts his arm round her waist*): Indru!
  Remember the girls.

BANYAN: Yes, remember the girls.

KALEE: We're only human, you know.

TIFFIN: And have our feelings.

INDRU: I'm very sorry, ladies; but, really, your habit of travelling in a crowd is most embarrassing. We don't at all mind being left alone, if you've anything on.

BANYAN: But we haven't.

INDRU: Now, if you really have any appointments anywhere, pray

BANYAN: We never make detached appointments.

TIFFIN: We couldn't think of leaving Beebee unprotected. Beebee wouldn't like it.

BEEBEE: No, I shouldn't like it. I should object.

KALEE: We couldn't turn our thoughts away from Beebee under any circumstances.

INDRU: But if you can't turn your thoughts away, you might see the propriety of turning your heads.

BEEBEE: Yes, girls, you might turn your heads.

BANYAN: If we are in the way you had better say so.

TIFFIN: We can take a hint.

INDRU: Oh, you can take a hint.

GIRLS: Yes.

INDRU: Then I wish to goodness you would take one. Take several; take a dozen; help yourself to as many as you like, and go!

Girls go off sulkily.

INDRU (*takes her by both hands*): Beebee, I have serious news. My father has discovered our secret. Oh, if you were only a Brahmin!

BEEBEE: I am; or rather, I was.

INDRU: I don't understand.

BEEBEE: Forty years ago my father, a respected Brahmin, was crossing a river; the boat capsized; a man on the bank threw a rope and hauled him ashore.

INDRU: And his life was saved?

BEEBEE: Yes; but his Caste was lost.

INDRU: How so?

BEEBEE: The man on the bank was a Pariah, and the Court held that the taint of dishonour was communicated from him to my father down the rope.

INDRU: What a pity he didn't slip on a pair of gloves before grasping it.

GEORGE DANCE AND FRANK DESPREZ

BEEBEE: He appealed against the decision, and the case has been pending ever since. We were once a wealthy family, but all our possessions have been squandered in Court fees and legal refreshers. It was to pay for Counsel's opinion on a technical point that I took an engagement as a Nautch dancer.

INDRU: Brave girl! But why this endless delay?

BEEBEE: We have been most unfortunate. First of all, one of the Jury died, and they had to go through it all again; then our Counsel took the scarlet fever; and then, to vary the monotony, the Counsel on the other side took the yellow fever. Then one of the officials absconded with the brief; then they lost the shorthand notes; and so it has gone on for forty years.

INDRU: And is the Court still sitting?

BEEBEE: Yes, or rather, it was. The Judge has got the influenza now.

INDRU: It will be unfortunate if anything should happen to him. They would have to go through it all again, wouldn't they?

BEEBEE: Don't! The very suggestion makes me feel quite giddy. (*Cross*)

INDRU: Do you think the case ever will end?

BEEBEE: I don't think it ever will. (*Sobs*)

INDRU (*confidentially*): Never mind we will be married all the same.

BEEBEE: Impossible!

INDRU: Nothing is impossible to those who love as we love. If you cannot come up to my level, I must come down to yours.

DUET. INDRU AND BEEBEE.

INDRU: When our shackles are undone,
　　　　When I breathe the word,
　　Wilt thou have this man, fair one,
　　　　To thy wedded lord?

BEEBEE: I will.

INDRU: Wilt thou honour and obey him,
　　　　Never hoodwink or betray him?
　　　　Wilt thou true allegiance pay him?

BEEBEE: I will.
　　　In sickness and health,
　　　In want and in wealth,
　　　　　I take thee for ever and ever.

Both: I take thee for ever and ever.

Beebee: When the gossip-tongue's astir
With the Nautch girl's life,
Wilt thou have this maiden, Sir,
To thy wedded wife?

Indru: I will.

Beebee: If unworthy they would make her,
If they ask thee to forsake her,
Wilt thou to thy bosom take her?

Indru: I will.
In sunshine and rain,
In peace and in pain,
I take thee for ever and ever.

Both: I take thee for ever and ever.

Enter Currie.

Currie: Still at it. Are you aware, young lady, that you are braving the terrors of the law?

Beebee: What have I done?

Currie: Well, when a Nautch girl aspires to the hand of a Prince, I think you will admit she's done something.

Beebee: But I was not aware of his rank when I fell in love with him.

Currie: Then you should have inquired. You don't expect a member of the Royal Family to go about with a crown on his head and a throne in his portmanteau, do you? Now see the result. The Rajah has ordered you to be brought before him for trial, and you will probably be sentenced to be thrown to the sacred crocodiles. (*Beebee cries*)

Indru (*aside to Beebee*): Be brave, Beebee. I will return in five minutes to claim you as my own, and not even the Rajah can then separate us. (*Exit*)

Currie (*earnestly*): I may be able to save you?

Beebee: Yes?

Currie: I have arranged to take my troupe to the Paris Exhibition, and am expecting the signed agreement every moment. A steamer sails in an hour's time, and if the contract arrives before then we can all get on board and escape.

Beebee: And leave Indru? No.

Currie: Foolish girl! Come with me not that way! (*Trying to pull her off*) Here comes the Rajah! (*He takes her off*)

GEORGE DANCE AND FRANK DESPREZ

Room for Punka! room for Punka!
　　Punka comes in royal state!
Clear the roadway! clear the roadway!
　　Punka comes, Punka the Great!
Crash the cymbal, beat the tom-tom,
　　Let the brazen trumpet roar;
Room for Punka, Royal Punka,
　　Rajah he of Chutneypore!
Enter Punka.

Recitative.

Punka: Oh, yes! oh, yes! oh, yes!
　　Know all men by these presents,
　　I'm the Rajah of Chutneypore!
Chorus: Punka, the Rajah of Chutneypore,
　　the Rajah of Chutneypore!

Song.

Punka: And this is the royal diadem
　　Of the Rajah of Chutneypore.
Chorus: Of Punka, of Punka, the Rajah of Chutneypore!
Punka: And this is the big ancestral gem
　　That decks the royal diadem
　　Of the Rajah of Chutneypore.
Chorus: Of Punka, of Punka, the Rajah of Chutneypore!
Punka: And this is the arm all cut and scored
　　That wields the sharp and trusty sword,
　　That guards the big ancestral gem
　　That decks the royal diadem
　　Of the Rajah of Chutneypore.
Chorus: Of Punka, of Punka, the Rajah of Chutneypore!
Punka: And this is the heart so staunch and true,
　　That nerves the eyes of hazel hue,
　　That steers the arm all cut and scored,
　　That wields the sharp and trusty sword,

That guards the big ancestral gem
That decks the royal diadem
Of the Rajah of Chutneypore.

CHORUS: Of Punka, of Punka, the Rajah of Chutneypore!

PUNKA: And this is the Prince, long may he reign,
That owns the clear and subtle brain,
That rules the heart so staunch and true,
That nerves the eyes of hazel hue,
That steers the arm all cut and scored,
That wields the sharp and trusty sword,
That guards the big ancestral gem
That decks the royal diadem
Of the Rajah of Chutneypore.

CHORUS: Of Punka, of Punka, the Rajah of Chutneypore!

PUNKA: And this is the patriotic lay
That's sung by lords and ladies gay
That serve the Prince, long may he reign,
That owns the clear and subtle brain,
That rules the heart so staunch and true,
That nerves the eyes of hazel hue,
That steers the arm all cut and scored,
That wields the sharp and trusty sword,
That guards the big ancestral gem
That decks the royal diadem
Of the Rajah of Chutneypore.

CHORUS: Of Punka, of Punka, the Rajah of Chutneypore!

PUNKA: Well, where is our cousin the active and intelligent Pyjama?

Enter Pyjama, followed by Beebee.

PUNKA: Oh, here you are! (*To Pyjama*) And where is this Nautch girl
who has dared to make love to our son? (*warming up*) this creature
who has, as it were, presumed, so to speak, even so much as to but
we'll take it as read. Where is she?

PYJAMA: Here, your Highness. (*Brings forward Beebee, who kneels*)

PUNKA: Ha! (*advances furiously towards her*) Now, young person, hold
up your head!

BANYAN: Poor Beebee!

PUNKA: Silence, or I'll clear the Court. (*To Beebee*) Hold up your
head! Hold up your head, I say! Will you hold up (*she looks up,
he suddenly melts and smiles at her*) How d'ye do? Warm isn't

GEORGE DANCE AND FRANK DESPREZ

it? (*Aside*) What a pretty face! I'm not at all surprised at Indru. How lovely!

PYJAMA (*stepping in front of him, admiring Beebee*): Charming!

PUNKA (*aside*): Now, were it not for the consanguinity existing between myself and that person, I should peremptorily order them to cleave him through the skull. (*Aloud*) Ahem! (*Pyjama moves Punka raises Beebee*) And so you love my little Indy, eh, pretty one?

BEEBEE: Yes, your Highness.

PUNKA: And did it not occur to you that such a presumption on the part of a Nautch girl would rouse the ire of the mildest monarch that ever lived?

BEEBEE: I was not aware of his exalted rank, your Highness, or I would not have dared to look at him.

PUNKA: I should think not, indeed. Our family are not only Brahmins, but Brahmins of the very finest vintage. We have been in bottle, so to speak, eighteen hundred years. I think I am justified in saying that you have not even a trace of blue in your veins.

BEEBEE: I don't know, your Highness.

PUNKA: Look at that! (*Gives paper*) It is a chemical analysis of our family blood, which, you will observe, yields one hundred and twenty grains of indigo to the square inch.

BEEBEE: How very blue it must be!

PUNKA: It is unusually blue.

PYJAMA (*idiotically*): I reckon one of us would be of incalculable value to a family who do their washing at home.

PUNKA (*to Pyjama, glaring at him*): Idiot! (*To Beebee*) You will now understand that the difference between my son's rank and your own is a complete bar to your union.

BEEBEE: I do, your Highness.

PUNKA: Then you are a sensible girl, and that fact will be taken into consideration when the Court proceeds to pass judgment upon you.

BEEBEE: I am conscious of my crime, your Highness, and at your feet I crave your mercy. (*Kneels, weeping*)

PUNKA (*aside*): How pretty she looks through her tears! (*Stooping over her*) Dry your eyes, sweet one, dry your eyes.

PYJAMA (*passing in front of him*): Allow me, miss.

PUNKA: Ahem! (*Pyjama falls back aside*) If he were not a relation (*Aloud*) In consideration of your deep contrition, you will merely be required to enter into your own recognizances for your future good conduct. The Court has been moved to take this lenient view of the case on account of the prisoner's extreme youth and beauty, and we wish it to go forth and possibly the gentlemen of the press will take note of it I say, we wish it to go forth, that if only the prisoner were a Brahmin, we should not be at all averse to receiving her into our family, either as a daughter or wife

PYJAMA (*embracing Beebee*): Or cousin.

PUNKA (*aside*): I shall certainly give that person a sound thrashing one day, relative or no relative. (*Aloud*) The prisoner leaves the Court without a stain on her character.

Exeunt to refrain of Chorus Pyjama, Beebee, Banyan, Kalee, Tiffin, and Chorus. Punka remains.

PUNKA: Thank goodness! they're all gone.

Chinna enters.

CHINNA: What, Rajah! all alone? You seem annoyed.

PUNKA: I believe I am the most unfortunate monarch on earth, and all owing to the pernicious influence of a certain phrenological bump. (*Feels skull*)

CHINNA: Nonsense!

PUNKA: No; not nonsense. Consanguinity there it is! (*Indicates the organ*)

CHINNA: There isn't such a bump.

PUNKA: There wasn't until I was born. I was the first to develop it. It is now over four years since I communicated my discovery to the Lancet; and they were good enough to christen the new organ, "Consanguinity, No. 39A."

CHINNA: And what has this to do with your ill fate?

PUNKA: Everything. If the love of kindred had not predominated in my composition to such an absurd degree, I should never have taken you and Pyjama from the gutter metaphorically speaking and put you in office at Court. From that unfortunate act all my troubles date; for no sooner had it become known that I was recognizing my poor relations, than cousins, half-cousins, quarter-cousins, and fractions of cousins turned up from every quarter of Hindustan; until at the present moment there isn't a single post in my kingdom to which a salary is attached that isn't held by one of them.

CHINNA: They ought to be grateful.

PUNKA: You catch them being grateful! They're always asking for something, and they're never satisfied until they've got it, and then they're not. Oh, I wish they were all in the crocodile pond.

CHINNA: Why doesn't your Majesty put them there with exceptions, of course. You have but to command your guards.

PUNKA: Yes, I can command my guards, but can I command my feelings? The rascals remind me that the "same blood flows in our veins." Ugh! I know they're a lot of sponging, treacherous humbugs, and yet the same old arguments always fetch me.

CHINNA: But, your Majesty

PUNKA: Don't interrupt, please. Then there's this bother about Indru and that tiresome business of the diamond too.

CHINNA: But that wasn't a relation's doing, was it?

PUNKA (*mysteriously*): It was. Ten years ago one of them, who shall be nameless (*looks off after Pyjama*)

CHINNA (*astonished*): Pyjama?

PUNKA: Never mind; whoever it was, he stole the diamond that formed the left eye of Bumbo, the Idol, and sold it to an Englishman, who travelled in curios for a London firm. We instantly despatched a High Priest and a couple of Thugs to recover the precious jewel. They pursued it through many vicissitudes, but missed it at every turn. They traced it first to the diamond merchant in Hatton Garden; but the day before they arrived, his safe had been broken open, and the diamond stolen by a well-to-do burglar, who, for better security, deposited it at his banker's whose head cashier promptly absconded with the Idol's eye in his portmanteau to Spain. On the journey, the train was robbed by a party of brigands, whose leader, a fine, fearless, free-shooting fellow, was about to start for the Spanish Exhibition at Earl's Court, of which he was to be one of the chief attractions. He ultimately became a lion of the London season, and gave the diamond to a Countess, whose husband, being dissatisfied with her story that she found it in the folds of her train after a scrimmage at a drawing-room at Buckingham Palace, flung it in a rage out of his back bed-room window into a mews, where it was picked up and swallowed by an enterprising Cochin China fowl, who was killed next day. It was discovered by the cook in dressing the bird; she gave it to a policeman, who gave it to a housemaid, who gave it to a Life-Guardsman, who gave it to a pretty parlour-maid, who gave it to a young gentleman just home from Eton, against whom she soon afterwards entered an action for breach of promise. After a vain attempt to convince the Court that his letters had been written by a foster-brother of whom he was the identical image, the youth fled with the diamond to other climes. He was last heard of in the interior of Africa, where he has evaded our emissaries, and twice escaped being "rescued" by private expeditions sent out by the English. Since then, all trace of him has been lost.

CHINNA: Then nothing can be done?

PUNKA: What more do you want? I am held responsible by the outraged Idol for the absence of his optic. The terror is always over me. You don't know what an irritable, despotic deity this Bumbo is. There's absolutely no knowing what he may take it into his head to do, or what time he may choose for doing it. Unless I can find the jewel, or find it in my heart to denounce a relative, I fear the worst.

CHINNA: But why did you not denounce the thief?

PUNKA: You know my unfortunate weakness. He fell on his knees and said, "Am I not your fifty-fifth cousin?" (*Aside*) Ah, here is the rascal!

Pyjama enters, bringing on Beebee.

PYJAMA: The young person has a communication to make.

BEEBEE: Your Highness was good enough to say that if I were a Brahmin you would accept me as your daughter

PUNKA: Or wife.

BEEBEE: I am of Brahmin descent, and am now petitioning the Court to restore my lost rank.

PUNKA: If you succeed, you may call at our Palace any Monday morning between ten and twelve; and if our son is by that time married, and we are still a widower, we will give you the refusal or our hand and heart.

BEEBEE: Your Majesty is too good.

PUNKA: Not at all. I have been looking for a wife for some time; you come up to my idea of what a wife should be; and as such, you would, I think, supply a long-felt want.

QUARTET. BEEBEE, CHINNA, PYJAMA, AND PUNKA.

PUNKA: Now, when a young man says, "I think
It's time I lost my heart,"

He ought to look around, I think,
    Before he throws the dart.
For model wives and true, I think,
Are far between and few, I think,
Though there are odd ones who, I think,
    Supply a long-felt want.
Not the bilious-headache person who sits moping in a chair,
Nor the Senior-Wrangler person with a stubble crop of hair,
Nor the Bloom of Ninon person whose face won't stand the
    weather,
But quite another different kind of person altogether.
ALL: Yes, quite another different kind of person altogether.
BEEBEE: And when a maiden says, "I think,
    I'll let him buy the ring,"
She ought to ask herself, I think,
    "Now, is he quite the thing?"
For model men and fair, I think,
Are very, very rare, I think,
Yet one may here and there, I think,
    Supply a long-felt want.
Not the third-class-smoking person who is colouring a clay,
Nor the ten-in-fifty person who plays billiards all the day,
Nor the tea-and-muffin person who will strike you with a
    feather,
But quite another different kind of person altogether.
ALL: Yes, quite another different kind of person altogether.
PYJAMA: This maxim will apply, I think,
    To old as well as young;
And when December woos, I think,
    He ought to guard his tongue.
For model wives and good, I think,
Are rare in widowhood, I think,
Yet there are some who would, I think,
    Supply a long-felt want.
Not the breach-of-promise person who salutes each man she sees,
Nor the House of Commons person who wants feminine M.P.'s,
Nor the Hallelujah person whose lungs are made of leather,
    But quite another different kind of person altogether.
ALL: Yes, quite another different kind of person altogether.

CHINNA: The sauce that suits the goose, I think,
    Should suit the gander too;
  And Joan should have a care, I think,
    When Darby comes to woo.
  For model men and old, I think,
  Are rare on earth as gold, I think,
  Though odd ones, I've been told, I think,
    Supply a long-felt want.
Not the sluggish-liver person who says just what he feels,
Nor the extra-special person who will read through all his meals,
  Nor the atmospheric person who changes with the weather,
  But quite another different kind of person altogether.
ALL: Yes, quite another different kind of person altogether.

DANCE.

Enter Indru, wearing the dress of an outcast.

PUNKA (*seeing Indru, who salaams*): Indru, what means this?

INDRU: I am no longer a Brahmin, your Majesty.

PUNKA: Is this a joke?

INDRU: No, sir. I have just eaten a small plate of potted cow in the Bazaar, and renounced my Caste. So now I may marry Beebee, sweet Beebee.

CHINNA (*aside*): To think that he should throw himself away like this; and just when it had suddenly struck me that he was the one person capable of making me happy!

PUNKA: What right have you to do such a thing? You have cut yourself off from me for ever.

CHINNA: And from me.

PYJAMA: And from me, and all your cousins.

INDRU: I can only plead my love in extenuation.

PUNKA: Here am I, in the autumn of life, without a son to cheer my declining years, without an heir to inherit my crown.
  What is to be done?

PYJAMA: May I suggest a scheme?

PUNKA: Have you a vested interest in it?

PYJAMA: Well, er yes, slightly.

PUNKA: I thought so. We don't want to hear it.

Exit Pyjama.

INDRU (*aside to Beebee*): I have prepared everything. They are waiting to marry us. Come!

Beebee and Indru steal off.
Punka sits, deeply depressed.

CHINNA (*coming up to him and putting her hand on his shoulder*):
Cheer up, Rajah! you're not the only unhappy being whose
feelings get the best of him. I, too, am a victim of irresistible
impulses.

PUNKA: You?

CHINNA: Since I was sixteen I have been seeking for an affinity,
that mysterious being who is waiting for me somehow,
somewhere.

PUNKA: Where?

CHINNA: I don't exactly know where.

PUNKA: Oh, I thought perhaps it was an appointment.

CHINNA: Whenever I meet him a thrill passes over me. I see nothing,
hear nothing, smell nothing, taste nothing, feel nothing.

PUNKA: I say, I say! That's very bad.

CHINNA: Please, don't interrupt me, Rajah. I mean, of course, except
him!

PUNKA: And are these indications invariably accurate?

CHINNA: Well, on one or two occasions, certainly I have mistaken the
symptoms, but I see you do not understand me.

SONG. CHINNA.
(*words by Frank Desprez*)

Do not think me over-bold,
    Though my sentiments are strong;
And my heart is far from cold
    Well, in that there's nothing wrong.
        I am seeking my divinity,
        My idol, my affinity;
And when I come across him as I often think I do
        I forget myself a minute,
        But there's really nothing in it.

PUNKA: Have you often had these "impulses"?

CHINNA: That's most unkind of you!
    I can't help it! Really no!
    Do not laugh 'tis truly so.

On each of these occasions,
These passing aberrations,
My heart goes out to meet him,
And my arms extend to greet him
To a kiss I'd almost treat him.
I can't help it!

These attacks, I'm glad to mention,
 Only last a little while,
I return to stern convention,
 To a sneer subdue my smile.
  Avoid familiarity,
  Snub ordinary charity,
And freeze him with a frown that keeps him
  off a yard or two.
  Atone for past frivolity
  By speech of coldest quality.

PUNKA: Do you often ice your manner?

CHINNA: Now that's much too bad of you!
 I can't help it, really no!
 Through the world I sadly go.
 I am seeking a divinity,
 And finding an affinity,
 My heart goes out to meet him -
 And my arms extend to greet him
 To a kiss I'd almost treat him.
  I can't help it!

Exit Chinna.

Pyjama enters.

PUNKA: Well, what is it now?

PYJAMA (*with suppressed delight*): I've some news for you, Beebee's action is finished. The Court has decided in her favour, and she in now a Brahmin.

PUNKA: A Brahmin! And just as Indru has renounced his Caste! Now, could there possibly be anything more exasperating.

PYJAMA: It certainly has its humorous side, hasn't it?

PUNKA: They're as far away from marriage as ever.

PYJAMA: Poor girl! But she sha'n't be disappointed of a wedding!

PUNKA: How so?

PYJAMA: I'll marry her myself.

Exit.

PUNKA: And I believe he would. I honestly think that man's capable of
anything.

Exit.

FINALE OF ACT I.

Enter Banyan, Kalee, Tiffin, Nautch Girls, Soldiers, and others.

ENSEMBLE.

WOMEN.	MEN.
Merrily, merrily peals the bell,	Ding, dong,
In the temple swinging;	Ding, dong, etc.
Merrily, merrily voices swell,	
Gladsome tidings bringing.	
Merrily, merrily press the crowd,	
From Beebee's wedding we come;	
Merrily, merrily chant aloud	
Her epithalamium.	

Enter Indru and Beebee.

BEEBEE: Beebee's a bride now, as every one knows,

INDRU: And Beebee's all blushes, just like a red rose.

BEEBEE: Beebee is trembling with maidenly fears,

INDRU: And Beebee is smiling, in spite of her tears.

BEEBEE: Beebee is glowing with womanly pride,

INDRU: And Beebee's the sweetest and handsomest bride.

BEEBEE: Beebee is beaming with conjugal mirth,

INDRU: And Beebee's the happiest creature on earth.

ENSEMBLE.

BEEBEE and INDRU.	CHORUS.
In sunshine and rain,	Beebee is glowing
In peace and in pain,	with womanly pride, etc.
I take thee for ever and ever.	

Punka and Pyjama have entered. Punka comes forward.

PUNKA: Oh, headstrong pair, your folly you will rue,
    The Court has issued its award, and you (*to Beebee*)
        Are now a Brahmin.
Gives paper pause horror of Indru and Beebee.
                  by the law's decree
    Your vows are void; his wife you ne'er can be.
ALL: Stop the merry marriage bell,
        Hush the joyous song;
      Toll instead the dolesome knell,
        Beat the mystic gong.
      Haul the silken banners down,
        Halt the pageant show;
      Doff the smile and don the frown,
        Chant the Hymn of Woe.
INDRU: What is Caste to you and me,
      Who live for love alone?
    To some country let us flee,
      Where no such ban is known.
    To some far-off happy land
      Beyond the Brahmin sway,
    We will journey hand in hand,
      To live and love for aye.
BEEBEE: Yes, yes, that happy land we'll find,
    And leave this hated Caste behind.
CHORUS: That happy, happy land they'll find,
    And leave this hated Caste behind.
PYJAMA: One moment pause. My conscience bids me throw
    A cloud across the sunshine of your hopes.
    It is decreed by Act of Punka Rex,
    Nineteen and Twenty, Cap. Eighteen, that when
    A Brahmin marries one of lower Caste,
    Together they shall die a traitor's death.
    And kinsfolk, loving kinsfolk though you be,
My conscience bids me go for the police.
Exit Pyjama.
ALL: Oh, cruel law! oh, harsh decree!
        Oh, statute born of fool!
      Oh, fiendish code! oh, carrion rite!
        Oh, legislative ghoul!

INDRU: Must we then die? Is there no hope left still?

BEEBEE: Will no one save us?

BOTH: Will no one save us?

CURRIE (*entering*): Yes, I can and will!
 The ship is waiting by the quay
 To bear my troupe across the sea.
 And here's the contract, which you'll find
 Is duly stamped and sealed and signed.

INDRU: Stamped,

BEEBEE: Sealed,

TRIO: Signed,

CURRIE: So come with me and join my band,
 And fly unto a foreign land,
 And say farewell for evermore
 To cross and cruel Chutneypore.

INDRU and BEEBEE: Yes, yes, we'll go.

CURRIE: Then do not longer wait.

INDRU (*to Punka*): Good-bye, farewell.

CURRIE: Quick, ere it is too late.

ENSEMBLE.

TIFFIN.	THE OTHERS.
Away, away,	Away, away
Ill-fated twain	Across the main,
Whose wedding day	Beyond the sway
Is born in pain;	Of Brahma's reign,
Seek some lone spot	Unto a spot
Far o'er the sea.	Far o'er the sea,
May such a lot	Where Caste is not
Ne'er come to me.	And men are free.

PUNKA.

Alas, a-day!
 My broad domain
Will pass away
 With Punka's reign,

A wretched lot
    My life will be,
  Son I have not,
     Ha, woe is me!

Currie hurries Beebee off. Indru is about to follow her when Pyjama enters with Soldiers, who arrest him.

Act II

The Courtyard of PUNKA's palace. A cell is seen, with grated window, in which Indru is confined. Suttee, Cheetah, and Poor Relations discovered.

OPENING CHORUS.

We are Punka's poor relations
    By a lucky zephyr blown
Up the easiest gradations
    From the gutter to the throne.
We have risen from the people
    By a mighty strength of will,
From the basement to the steeple,
    From the valley to the hill.
We are Punka's poor relations, etc.
Enter Chinna.

SOLO. CHINNA.

Twelve months have scarcely journeyed by
Since we were of the common fry,
Housemaids, scullions, cooks, and nurses,
Governesses, teachers, nurses,
Toiling, broiling, day by day
In a common, humdrum way
CHORUS: Quite a common, humdrum way.
CHINNA: When Punka driven into meekness,
    By some strange phrenologic weakness,
    Summoned all his poor relations
    From their low and humble stations,
    Gave them posts about his throne,
    And bade them make his home their own.
CHORUS: We quickly made his home our own.
CHINNA: And now our cousin rues the hour
    When he invested us with power.
    We rule the roast. For truth to tell
    He gave an inch, we took an ell.

SUTTEE: Yes, yes, we took several ells.

CHEETAH: An unlimited number of ells.

CHORUS: Millions, and billions, and trillions,
    quadrillions, and also quintillions of ells!

CHINNA: And now we are ladies attached to the Court,
    The highly-exclusive and towering sort;
    With pinnacle people we only resort,
        Like the high-top-gallant ladies
    that we are.

CHORUS: Yes, now we are ladies, etc.

We are Punka's poor relations, etc.

Enter Pyjama at back.

PYJAMA: Well, cousins, the Court has pronounced its sentence.
    Indru is to die to-morrow.

CHINNA: To-morrow! (*Aside*) I am only just in time.

CHEETAH: After lying six months in that prison! (*Pointing*) Poor
    fellow!

SUTTEE: Poor Beebee!

CHINNA (*contemptuously*): Beebee! Who thinks of Beebee now?
    Since she and Currie's troupe escaped to Europe, they have been
    forgotten.

CHEETAH: We have read of them in the papers, and heard what
    successes they made in Paris and London.

SUTTEE: And what a lot of beautiful presents were sent them!

PYJAMA: Never mind about Beebee! Listen; I have communicated
    the facts about Indru and Punka in an anonymous letter to the
    Idol Bumbo, which I have laid on his shrine. When he learns
    that Punka is the father of a condemned outcast, he will certainly
    sentence him to die also! (*Chuckling*)

CHINNA: And then you expect to be made Rajah! I know! (*Goes up and
    gets off during song*)

CHEETAH: You seem to have arranged things splendidly for yourself as
    usual.

PYJAMA: Would you like to know the secret of my luck?

CHEETAH and SUTTEE: We should.

GIRLS: Yes.

Song. Pyjama.

The secret of my past success is simple in its way:
I carefully avoid unlucky actions night and day.
I never pared my finger-nails on Friday in my life;
I'd rather cross the river Styx than cross a table-knife;
I never from my house turned out a black-haired pussy-cat;
    And when I meet a squint-eyed girl I always go like that!
And if I see a hunch-back pass, I touch him when I'm able,
And never since the innocent days of my childhood have
    I ever so far forgotten myself as to put my boots upon
    the table.

Chorus: And never since the innocent days of his childhood, etc.

    'Gainst thirteen round a table I instinctively revolt;
"Self-help" is e'er my motto if I'm asked to give some salt;
    I wouldn't see a new moon through a glass for anything;
    I always turn my money when I hear the cuckoo sing;
    I never, never pass another person on the stairs,
    Nor poke a fire unless I've known the owner seven years;
    I never whistle in a room, for nothing could be madder,
And I invariably step out into the roadway and risk amputation by
    the wheels of a passing vehicle than walk beneath a painter's
    ladder.

Chorus: And he invariably steps out, etc.

    I'm always very careful not to break a looking-glass;
And when the train's going o'er a bridge beneath I never pass;
    I wouldn't wear a peacock's feather on my hat, oh, no!
    Nor into a new domicile on Friday ever go.
    And when I make a present, I by no chance give a knife;
I've never stepped from bed upon the wrong side in my life;
    Than rather meet a funeral, I'd curl up in the gutter,
And be the craving of the inner man ever so acute, no living soul
    could on any account prevail upon me to take the last piece of
    bread-and-butter.

Chorus: And be the craving of the inner man, etc.

    When shaking hands I'm very, very careful not to cross;
    I always wish for something when I meet a piebald "hoss";
    I wouldn't open an umbrella in a room for gold,
    Nor have a baby photographed before it's six months old;

On Twelfth-cake Day the mistletoe must always
disappear,
And I engage a dark man to let in the glad new year;
A black pin I would never use, for nothing could be bolder,
And if, in an unguarded moment, I'm ever betrayed into
committing any of the aforementioned offences,
I immediately propitiate the Fates by simply turning
round three times, and tossing a pinch of salt over my
left shoulder.

CHORUS: And if, in an unguarded moment, etc.

PYJAMA: Now, cousins, let us go and book some seats for Indru's
execution to-morrow.

Pyjama and others exeunt. Chinna re-renters from back.

CHINNA: At last they're gone now is my chance. The bar and the
disguise that I have hidden (*looks for them behind column*) both
safe! Indru my affinity that is, my latest affinity you can now
escape!

DUET. CHINNA AND INDRU.
(*words by George Dance and Frank Desprez*)

CHINNA: A little caged bird below
A palace window hung;
His weary heart was crushed with woe,
And mute his silver tongue;
And every morn his faithful mate
Came from her lonesome nest,
And sang outside his prison-gate
The song he loved the best.

I'm waiting here below, she sang;
Why do you linger so? she sang;
'Tis I, my love, 'tis I, she sang,
And waited his reply. (*Listens*)

INDRU: I come oh, do not go, my love;
The hours seem sad and slow, my love;
I'm weary of this woe, ny love,
A captive held am I!

Indru: Well, pretty Chinna, have you come once more
 To cheer the captive with your tuneful strain;
 Useless your thought for such a wretch as I;
 To-morrow yes, to-morrow I must die!
Chinna: I've come to save you from your fate.
Indru: But how
 Save me? Alas! how can you save me now?
Chinna (*showing it*):
 This bar of steel will break your prison-bars.
Indru: 'Tis heavy; you can hardly lift its weight!
Chinna: How can we get it up? Ah! let down straight
 Your turban. (*He does so*)
Indru: Clever girl!
Chinna: Haul up!
Indru: I do!
Chinna: Take that bar of trusty steel,
 Ply it with a lusty zeal,
 Burst your bonds, and you are free,
 Oh, delicious liberty!
Indru (*as he breaks bar*): Again, again,
 Each muscle I strain!
 The mortar is old!
  The bricks will not break!
  No, no, they shake!
 They quiver, they bend!
 My task's at an end!
 'Tis done! I'm free! (*comes down*)
 Thanks, Chinna, to thee!
He gets out, and down stage.
Chinna and Indru: What joy to him/her, what joy to me!
 What happiness to break his/one's chain!
 Oh, welcome, sweetest liberty!
 He's/I'm free again, he's/I'm free again!
Indru: And now, dear Chinna, I must fly.
Chinna: Not so!
 You must not in that garb attempt to go.
 Here (*showing it*) is a dress in which, when once disguised,

You will not, I believe, be recognized!

INDRU: Is there aught more?

CHINNA: Nothing unless
    You

INDRU: What?

CHINNA (*aside*): How dense men are! (*aloud*) Why, can't you guess?
    I want to leave this hateful Chutneypore,
    And never see its dark walls any more.
    Beebee has left you she is not your wife
    And, if you asked me to be yours for life,
    Perhaps I'd not refuse;
    I say, perhaps I'd not refuse.

INDRU: What can I say?
    Would that this heart were mine to give away!
    And then but, no Beebee is still my own,
    And, though we're parted, I am hers alone!

CHINNA: This is the old, old story! Jack is in love with Jill;
    Jill doesn't care for Johnnie, but deeply adoreth Bill;
    Bill worships dainty Dorothy Dorothy, trim and tall,
    Is pining and burning for Dick, who is yearning
    For Cis, who loves no one at all.

BOTH: This is the old, old story! etc.

CHINNA (*aside*): Another disappointment. Well, I'm used to it.
    Sooner or later I shall find him later probably.

    (*Aloud*) But you've no time to lose on with that disguise, and

INDRU (*pointing off R*): Look, my father! I must say farewell to him.

CHINNA: Impossible! (*Pointing L*) See! That horrid Pyjama. He will
    certainly betray you! Round this corner, quick!

Exit Indru.

CHINNA: The next time I find my affinity there shall be no mistake
    about it.

Exit Chinna.

Enter Punka, pensively, R.

PUNKA: More troubles!

Enter Pyjama, running.

PYJAMA: Have you heard the news?

PUNKA: What news?

PYJAMA: Of Bumbo the Idol?

PUNKA: Bumbo?

PYJAMA: He has come to life.

PUNKA: Ha! That's so like him. Just the sort of thing he would do. Pure aggravation!

PYJAMA: Yes. (*Melodramatic music*) As one of the Priests of the Temple was dusting him this morning, he noticed a wave of animation slowly passing over his face.

PUNKA: Ha!

PYJAMA: His lips quivered, his nostrils dilated, and then his one eye slowly opened like the moon emerging from a cloud.

PUNKA: Ha!

PYJAMA: He gave one mighty shiver, stretched his arms, yawned three times, and, after wiping a cobweb from the corner of his eye, stepped from the shelf on which he has been sitting for two thousand years. (*Music stops*)

PUNKA: What's he doing now?

PYJAMA: He is coming here!

Exeunt separately.

Enter Suttee, Cheetah, Poor Relations, and Priests.

CHORUS.

PRIESTS: Oh, ye people! Oh, ye people!
          Cast yourselves upon the earth, ye people!
     Grovel, grovel, creep and grovel,
          So confess your humble worth, ye people!
GIRLS: Bumbo comes! The mighty Bumbo!
          Brahma's idol, great and just, ye people!
     Grovel, grovel, man and maiden,
          Bow the head and lick the dust!

Enter Bumbo, carried on by Priests in a sedan chair. The doors are suddenly thrown open, and he steps out. He has the appearance of having been recently gilded and varnished, and wears a green shade over his left eye.

RECITATIVE. BUMBO.

'Tis well! 'tis well! Your piety I praise,
   Remain and bask in mighty Bumbo's rays.
You marvel doubtless at my animation,
   I'll condescend e'en to an explanation.

Song. Bumbo.
(*words by Frank Desprez*)

As I sat on my shelf, alone all by myself,
    What Idol so happy as I?
I could see what went on, who had come, who was gone,
    And the slightest omission espy.
Not an offering placed on the altar that graced
    My temple was ever unseen,
Though my right eye was dim, yet the fellow to him
    Was a gem of the purest, serene.
    And how do you think,
        The trouble arose,
    That left me no wink
        Of my pleasant repose?
CHORUS: It was all his eye!
BUMBO: It was all my eye,
CHORUS: The diamond eye,
BUMBO: My diamond eye,
CHORUS: It was all his eye,
BUMBO: My brilliant eye!
CHORUS: The diamond eye of the Idol!
BUMBO: One day to the shrine which you visit as mine
    There came an irreverent tramp,
  And quick as a rocket, my eye from its socket
    He whipped 'twas the left, too, the scamp!
  You often may wonder what's causing the thunder,
    Though cloudless the heavens may be;
  Don't notice the rumbling, it's only me grumbling
    To think that the villain's still free.
    And why do I rage,
        Vituperate,
    What is the reason
        My wrath's so great?
CHORUS: It's all his eye,
BUMBO: It's all my eye,
CHORUS: The diamond eye,
BUMBO: The brilliant eye,
CHORUS: It was all his eye,

BUMBO: My long-lost eye,

CHORUS: The diamond eye of the Idol!

(the following appears in the vocal score but not in the libretto)

BUMBO: With the Idol half blind, the priests didn't mind,
    Their indifference soon was habitual;
  There were nice goings on, all respect soon was gone,
    There was no sort of regular ritual.
  They forgot all their places, perhaps they made faces,
    And once, to my keen irritation,
  A rude devotee intruded on me
    In a state of perfect prostration.
  I blinked like a bat, but there as I sat
    I discovered by various senses
  I was being defrauded, imposed on, marauded,
    And cheated by falsest pretenses.
  The flowers in my lap had been under the tap,
    To endow them with shabby vitality,
  And the incense that burned I indignantly spurned
    It was hundred-and-second rate quality.
    Cower in fear!
        Ye guilty quake!
    Why am I here?
        Revenge to take!

CHORUS: It's all his eye,

BUMBO: It's all my eye,

CHORUS: The diamond eye,

BUMBO: The diamond eye,

CHORUS: It was all his eye,

BUMBO: My long-lost eye, my envied eye,
  My kidnapped eye, my precious eye,
  My brilliant eye,

BUMBO and CHORUS: The diamond eye of the Idol!

BUMBO (*to* PUNKA): Well, Punka, you didn't expect me, eh? Have you
    made your will?

PUNKA: My will?

BUMBO: You're very dense this morning! I'll put it another way. Have
    you anything to say why sentence of death should not be passed
    upon you?

PUNKA: Sentence of death? My dear boy.

BUMBO: Don't address me as your dear boy. I'm not a boy; I celebrated my two-thousandth birthday last week.

PUNKA: But

BUMBO: Silence! You have a son who a few month ago renounced his Caste by eating potted cow?

PUNKA: Potted cow? But that's not me!

BUMBO: The enactment is retrospective. The same cow I mean the same blood runs

PUNKA: Not that argument; I can't bear it! I hear it so often.

BUMBO: He has been sentenced to death for marrying out of his Caste. A felon's father cannot reign here. You have violated the sanctity of the throne.

PUNKA: But, surely, you attach no weight to the mad actions of a love-smitten youth?

BUMBO: I attach a weight to anything that serves my purpose. I shall presently attach a weight to your neck, preparatory to hurling you into the crocodiles' pond.

PYJAMA: Hear, hear!

POOR RELATIONS: Hear, hear!

PRIESTS: Hear, hear!

BUMBO: And then (*savagely*) what about my eye?

PUNKA: How could I prevent some person (*Looking at Pyjama, who winces*), who shall be nameless, from stealing it? I have acted as your guardian for many years, and, with this exception, you will allow I have proved faithful to my trust?

BUMBO: I allow nothing!

PUNKA: I took you from my father on a repairing lease, didn't I?

BUMBO: You did.

PUNKA: And I have done all to you that has been necessary, have I not?

BUMBO: In a jerry-built way, yes.

PUNKA: Haven't I had you insured against fire for three times your value?

BUMBO: After quietly abstracting the premium from the missionary-box.

PUNKA: When once a party of British tourists cut their initials on your nose, didn't I immediately have them obliterated?

BUMBO: With putty ugh! I can smell it now!

PUNKA: Didn't I have you painted and gilded up two years ago?

BUMBO: Not gilded, Dutch-metalled.

PUNKA: And give you three coats of the best oak varnish in the spring?

BUMBO: You did, and I've been sticky ever since, confound you! I'm a perfect catch-'em-alive-oh! Where is your son?

PUNKA: In yonder prison.

BUMBO: Produce him!

PYJAMA: Ha, look! (*Points to bars*) The bars are forced! The prisoner has flown!

BUMBO: Guard the city gates! (*To* PUNKA) You are Rajah no longer. Go, exchange that royal robe for the garb of an outcast, and return here prepared for your doom!

PUNKA: Would you leave the people without a leader?

PYJAMA (*stepping forward*): Don't make yourself anxious about that. (*To Bumbo*) As Grand Vizier, I understand the duties of Rajah well, and am quite prepared to accept the situation on the usual salary.

PUNKA: Ungrateful dog!

BUMBO: Take him away!

Exit Punka guarded.

BUMBO (*to Pyjama*): I appoint you Rajah in his stead. Within half an hour you will throw them, father and son, into the sacred water.

PYJAMA: Your commands shall be obeyed.

BUMBO: Mind they are! You can't deceive me. The moment they are seized by the hungry reptiles I shall be made aware of the fact by a pleasant tickling sensation on the soles of my feet, and if that titillation be delayed one instant beyond the stated time, then beware of the vengeance of the mighty Bumbo! (*Aside*) Have I done wisely in returning to life? Will they obey and respect me as before? May not some of the mysterious reverence which attaches to me Bah! This is weakness! But I have heard of so many idols, private and public, relegated to oblivion and neglect.

SONG. BUMBO.
(*words by Frank Desprez*)

When a fashionable tenor in his fascinating way,
Unutterably yearning, just evades his upper A;
Then ladies of all ages sit and simper, stare and sigh,
And adore his locks luxuriant and deep and rolling eye;
But as middle age approaches, and he takes to singing flat,
And is getting rather bald, and unromantically fat,
Then they transfer their devotion to some adolescent elf,

They have found another Idol that one's put upon the shelf.
Chorus: They have found another Idol, etc.
(this second verse appears in the vocal score but not in the libretto)

When an artist introduces us to art that's Japanese,

Before his cordless eyeglass we are down upon our knees,
And his pictures "spite all strictures" take the fancy of the town,
Sweetest "symphonies in amber," beauteous "harmonies in brown."

But a critic analytic gives the rhapsodist a rap,

And some other lad's invented by some other artist chap,

Then the pretty thing of porcelain is voted common delf,

And we get another Idol, that one's put upon the shelf.
Chorus: And we get another Idol, etc.

When a trav'ller equatorial returns from foreign parts,

With a manner dictatorial, and photographs and charts,

They list in rapt attention to the tales he has to tell,
And they dine him, and they wine him, and they marry him as well.
Then come rumours, and ill-humours tales of quite another kind,

As to comrades half-deserted, and contingents left behind;

And that traveller, indignant, writes and justifies himself,
But well, they get another Idol that one's put upon the shelf.
Chorus: Well, they get another Idol, etc.
Bumbo: Now, let my commands be obeyed, and leave me.

HYMN TO BUMBO. CHINNA, SUTTEE, CHEETAH, PYJAMA,
and CHORUS.

Hail, Bumbo!
Bumbo the Mentor!
Guardian of the Sun, and of the Moon, and of the Twinkling Stars!
Curator of the Brooks, the Rivers, and the Rolling Seas!
Hail, Bumbo, hail!
Ruler of the Beasts, Custodian of the Birds, and Commander-in-
chief of the Little Fishes!
Chief Librarian of the Book of Fate, and Responsible Managing
Director of the Wheel of Fortune!
Hail, Bumbo, hail!
Exeunt all but Bumbo.
Bumbo: I think I have done an excellent morning's work.
Enter Chinna.

GEORGE DANCE AND FRANK DESPREZ

Chinna (*aside*): Then it is true. The Idol has really come to life. (*Looks at Bumbo*) He's not so very bad looking. (*Then, with a sudden shock*) Ah!

Bumbo (*aside*): What a nice little person! (*Aloud*) Excuse me is anything the matter? May I?

Chinna (*aside, feeling her heart*): Is it? . . . Can it be? . . . Impossible. . . And yet. . . the symptoms are all ere. He's not at all bad-looking an idol a deity.

What am I to think?

Bumbo: What is your name, little one?

Chinna: Chinna Loofa.

Bumbo: How sweet! Married?

Chinna: Not as yet.

Bumbo: How fortunate! (*Takes her chin*)

Chinna: Please don't do that, sir.

Bumbo: Have no fear. Remember I am made of wood. I am perfectly harmless, I assure you. How would you like to be an Idol's bride, eh, pretty one?

Chinna (*aside*): It's all right this time!

Bumbo: And sit on a shelf?

Chinna: Oh, sir!

Bumbo: Would not the situation be novel?

Chinna: Oh no, I've been there eighteen months.

Bumbo: Where?

Chinna (*sighing*): On the shelf.

Bumbo: Not on mine. (*Pause*) Well, what do you say?

Chinna (*aloud, throwing herself into his arms*): My heart has spoken. I am yours.

Bumbo (*aside*): Generous readiness! (*Aloud*) By the bye, before we go any further, we had better understand each other clearly.

Chinna (*on his breast softly*): Settlements?

Bumbo: No.

Chinna: Oh!

Bumbo: You are aware that marriage isn't what it was?

Chinna: I am aware of the danger, nay, the positive wickedness, of incurring the bitterness of a baulked individuality; and, what's more, I don't intend to.

Bumbo: And of the necessity of self-development at any price?

Chinna: And of the "absurdity of living with a strange man."

BUMBO (*starting suspiciously*): Eh, you don't mean me?

CHINNA: Well, you are a little peculiar.

BUMBO: It runs in the family.

CHINNA: Heredity?

BUMBO: Exactly. So you think we shall suit each other?

CHINNA: Down to the ground. Our views of matrimony are so rational.

BUMBO: Not to say revolutionary.

DUET and COMIC CARMAGNOLE. CHINNA and BUMBO.
(*written by Frank Desprez*)

BUMBO: I shall flirt and fandangle though people may talk,
BOTH: Vive, vive la liberté!
BUMBO: Nor my idiosyncrasy banefully balk,
BOTH: Vive, vive la liberté!
BUMBO: I shall find my affinities just where I please
BOTH: Vive, vive la liberté!
BUMBO: And if you object I shall use Ibsenese!
　　Vive, vive la liberté!
CHINNA: Vive, vive,
　　V'là ce qu'arrive,
　　Vive, vive,
　　La liberté!
BOTH: Vive, vive, etc.
CHINNA: I shall dance with whomever I like barring you,
BOTH: Vive, vive la liberté!
CHINNA: And have hangers-on, say a dozen or two,
BOTH: Vive, vive la liberté!
CHINNA: I shall go out at night, though your leave you begrudge
BOTH: Vive, vive la liberté!
CHINNA: And if you prevent me I'll speak to a Judge,
BOTH: Vive, vive la liberté!
　　Vive, vive, etc.
BUMBO: But one thing occurs at this moment to me,
BOTH: Vive, vive la liberté!
CHINNA: I think I can guess it your meaning I see
BOTH: Vive, vive la liberté!
BUMBO: If the fetters of wedlock so lightly enthrall

BOTH: Vive, vive la liberté!

CHINNA: Is it really worth while to get married at all?

BOTH: Vive, vive la liberté!

BUMBO: Vive, vive,

CHINNA: French, I believe ah!

BOTH: Vive, vive,

La liberté!

BUMBO: Permit me. (*Offers his arm; they turn and meet Punka, who enters from back, wearing an outcast's dress*) You are prepared for your doom, I see.

PUNKA: Yes; excuse me, there's a blue-bottle on the tip of your (*pats fly on his nose*)

BUMBO (*pushing him away*): Don't maul me about! Wherever you touch you leave a finger-mark, and I don't like it.

PUNKA: And would you, in cold blood, condemn my son and myself to a horrible death?

BUMBO: My only regret is that there are no more of you. If you had a lot of relatives, this would be the happiest day of my life. (*Moves away with Chinna*)

PUNKA (*aside, breathing heavily, as though wrestling with his conscience*): Yes, yes, yes! Like a worm, you may tread upon a phrenological bump until it turns. (*To Bumbo, eagerly*) I have some relations cousins hundreds of them!

BUMBO: Good! We'll have a glorious execution this afternoon. I condemn them all to death!

CHINNA (*alarmed*): Ah!

BUMBO: All!

PUNKA: Including the half-cousins, the quarters, and the fractions?

BUMBO: Yes.

PUNKA (*aside, gloating*): Ha, ha, ha! Pyjama is one of the fractions. I look forward to the ceremony with a degree of gratification that is absolutely diabolical.

During this last speech Chinna is seen to converse with BUMBO *aside, and obtain from him an assurance that she will be exempt from the sentence.*

TRIO. CHINNA, BUMBO, and PUNKA.

PUNKA: You will sign our death-warrant to-day?

BUMBO (*angrily*): Of course

CHINNA (*aside*): But you won't include my name, I pray?

BUMBO (*aside, sweetly*): Of course.

PUNKA: And ere set of sun
    The deed will be done,
  In the regular, orthodox way?

BUMBO: Of course.

PUNKA: You'll indict us all in the decree?

BUMBO: Of course.

CHINNA (*aside*): But you'll make an exception of me?

BUMBO (*aside*): Of course.

PUNKA: You say you prefer,
    The homicide per
      C R O C O D I L E.

BUMBO: Of course.

PUNKA: C

BUMBO: R

CHINNA: O

PUNKA: C

BUMBO: O

CHINNA: D

PUNKA: I

BUMBO: L

PUNKA: E.

BUMBO (*giggling*): He! He!

PUNKA: In agony I will cheerfully die
    If locked in a cousin's caress,
  And that is the why and the what and the wherefore,
    The when and the nevertheless.

ALL: Yes, that is the why, etc.

BUMBO: Of course.

DANCE.

PUNKA: You will chain us all up in a row?

BUMBO: Of course.

CHINNA (*aside*): With a single exception, you know.

BUMBO (*aside*): Of course.

PUNKA: And then with a grin,
    You'll push us all in
  To the crocodiles waiting below?

BUMBO (*chuckling*): Of course,

To the crocodiles waiting below.

CHINNA: Of course.

PUNKA: You will watch our death-struggles with glee?

BUMBO: Of course.

CHINNA (*aside*): But you won't get the least glimpse of me.

BUMBO: Of course.

PUNKA: 'Twill make a rare stir,
  This massacre per
   C R O C O D I L E.

BUMBO: Of course.

PUNKA: C

BUMBO: R

CHINNA: O

PUNKA: C

BUMBO: O

CHINNA: D

PUNKA: I

BUMBO: L

PUNKA: E.

BUMBO: He! He!

PUNKA: I'll lie in the jaws of an alligator,
  And smile at my cousins' distress,
 And that is the why and the what and the wherefore,
  The when and the nevertheless.

ALL: He'll/I'll lie in the jaws of an alligator, etc.

Exeunt, dancing.

Enter Beebee.

SONG. BEEBEE.

Near thee once more; oh, sweet delight
To look again on eyes so bright,
To sing once more the hallowed lays,
The love songs of the bygone days!
Near thee once more,
Near thee once more.

From her hive the bee each morning
  Wings her way across the sward,

All the sweets at home discarding
    For the newer ones abroad.
From the sunflower to the lily,
    Sipping, sipping as she goes,
From the lily to the iris,
    From the iris to the rose;
Kissing here, kissing there,
Kissing, kissing everywhere.
The newest honey is the sweetest,
    And blissful is the quest,
The newest pleasures the completest,
    The newest love the best.

But when wintry winds are blowing,
    And the flowers are no more,
Then the bee in search of honey
    Turns unto the garnered store;
Gone the sunflower, gone the lily,
    Fickle sweethearts, faithless beaux;
Gone the lily, gone the iris,
    Gone the iris, gone the rose.
Faithless here, faithless there,
Faithless, faithless everywhere.
The old, old honey is the sweetest,
    And vain the fitful quest,
The old, old pleasure's the completest,
    The old, old love the best!

BEEBEE: At last I am back at the old spot. I shall never forget that dreadful moment after we sailed, when I discovered that Indru was not on board, and that every breath of wind bore me farther from him. Where can he be?

Enter at back Indru, disguised.

INDRU: I am trapped! The city gates are guarded, and even in this disguise, my features would be recognized. (*Sees Beebee*) Beebee!

BEEBEE: Indru! (*They embrace*)

INDRU: But where is Currie, and all the girls?

BEEBEE: Currie is here, but nearly all the girls have accepted other engagements in Europe.

INDRU: What a pity! But my Beebee has been true to me she has returned!

BEEBEE: Yes.

INDRU: You have brought no one's heart away?

BEEBEE: I have brought nothing but this gem. (*Indicating pendant at her neck*)

INDRU: What a brilliant stone! How curiously it is cut!

BEEBEE: It was said to be a charm that would give good fortune to her who carried it.

INDRU: Alas, Beebee! It has not bestowed it yet.

SONG. INDRU with BEEBEE.

When all the world was bright, love,
    And every night was day,
And all our thoughts were light, love,
    And all our work was play,
We smiled, and smiled again, love,
    At others' hapless lot,
We thought there was no pain, love,
    Because we felt it not.
The earth was green, and blue the sea,
The world was bright to you and me.

BOTH: The earth was green, etc.

INDRU: Now all the world is dark, love,
    And every day is night,
And dying is the spark, love,
    That once was shining bright.
The sun will never more, love,
    Rise from his golden bed,
To light us as of yore, love,
    For all the world is dead.

BOTH: For all the world is dead.

INDRU: The earth is bare, and black the sea,
The world is dead to you and me.

BOTH: The earth is bare, etc.

Enter Punka, guarded, with large scroll.

PUNKA: I can't find Pyjama. (*Seeing Indru*) You still here, and what Beebee! (*To Beebee*) Have you returned to contemplate the misery you have caused?

BEEBEE: No, great Rajah.

PUNKA: Don't address me as Rajah.

BEEBEE: Why not?

PUNKA: Well, I'd Rajah you didn't! I and Indru are both condemned. Pyjama's Rajah now.

BEEBEE: Is there no hope of escape?

PUNKA: None whatever. Besides, I am now really resigned to my fate. I don't think I want to escape. Look at that! (*Unfolds scroll*) Such an exquisite joke of mine!

INDRU: What is it?

PUNKA: A complete list of my relatives, three-hundred-and-seventy-four all told. I have persuaded the far-seeing Bumbo to extend his sentence to the cousins. He doesn't know that his new Rajah, Pyjama, is one of them. Ha! ha! ha!

BEEBEE: But if you could escape, you would still have the gratification of knowing they were dead.

PUNKA: But I shouldn't have the gratification of seeing them die. I wouldn't miss the sight for anything. The pleasure won't last long, I know; but it will be delicious while it's on.

INDRU: Would you sacrifice your life for the sake of a joke?

PUNKA: I'm not sure that I wouldn't. It's the first joke I've ever made, and I think a lot of it. The ornamental water is now being baited with penny buns and other appetizing crocodile hors d'œuvres, and by three o'clock it will literally swarm with the sacred saurians, at which hour the whole three-hundred-and-seventy-four of us will be chained together, myself at one end and Pyjama at the other. Bumbo has kindly promised to personally conduct the funeral service, which will be musical throughout; and at a given signal the whole string of us will be pitched into the water Pyjama's end goes in first. Ha! ha! ha!

Currie, Banyan, Kalee, and Tiffin have come on listening.

BEEBEE: Your Majesty must not sacrifice your valuable life to an exaggerated sense of humour. Ah! there is Currie he will help us! (*To Currie*) Do let us try and get to Europe again, and smuggle these two with us!

CURRIE: Now what is the good of asking me to do that? I can't go to Europe without a troupe. Where's my troupe? Gone! Scattered! All my prettiest girls have deserted me!

INDRU: Not the prettiest! They have returned.

BANYAN: I quite agree with you.

TIFFIN: So do I.

KALEE: And so do I.

BANYAN: There are three of us left, and not the least talented.

TIFFIN: Nor the least beautiful.

CURRIE: What's the use of three? You can't have a ballet of three you
    can't even have a front row of three and the public know so much
    nowadays, I don't think they'd even stand a quartette of three.

PUNKA: If you take us two, you can have a quartette of five. (*Indicating
    Indru, himself, and the three girls*) That ought to settle them!

CURRIE: Nonsense! What could you do? They've got enough
    ex-monarchs in Europe already you wouldn't draw!

INDRU: Why shouldn't we dance?

CURRIE: Because you don't know how.

BEEBEE: Oh, Indru dances exceedingly well. I've given him several
    lessons already.

PUNKA: Oh, I can dance. Look here!

CURRIE: You'll have to learn a great deal more than that. If we get
    back to Europe I shall introduce a novelty. The second part of
    our entertainment will consist of the dances of each country we
    visit, given by Baboo Currie's celebrated Nautch Troupe. There's a
    sensation for you!

SONG and DANCE. CURRIE, with BEEBEE, BANYAN, TIFFIN,
KALEE, INDRU, and PUNKA.
(*words by Frank Desprez*)

CURRIE: If we travel by way of Brindisi,
        Cross the Continent, get to Berlin,
    We must do and must dance just as we see
        The folk of the country we're in.
    In the valse with its airy attraction
        We'll affect to find infinite bliss,
    And drive Deutschers straight to distraction
        By elegant actions like this
Dances valse as he sings refrain.
    Round, round, ever around,
    Toes just touching the ground,
    Head bent, languishinglee
    That's how they do it in Germanee!

ALL: Round, round, ever around, etc.
German waltz.
CURRIE: When halting at giddy Gibraltar,
    Or stopping at sunny Cadiz,
  Your style will immediately alter,
      Turn your toes and attention to this
          (*strikes cachuca attitude*)
  To boleros your mind you'll abandon,
      And without any trouble or fuss,
      The light castanet lay your hand on,
          And conduct yourself cleverly thus
              (*Does cachuca*)
          Slide, slide, recede and advance,
          Flirt fan, prettily prance, (*kneels*)
          Swing arms again and again,
          That's how they do it in sunny Spain.
ALL: Slide, slide, recede and advance, etc.
Cachucha.
CURRIE: In London a little while stopt,
    In the mad metropolitan maze,
  With alacrity then you'll adopt
      The latest society craze.
  To don the "accordion pleat"
      Does every young lady prepare,
  And does wonderful things with her feet,
      Though old-fashioned people may stare.
He mimics skirt dancer à la Guards' Burlesque.
    Arms high, skirts lifted so,
    Head back, well-pointed toe,
    Neat hose, attitude free,
    That's how they do in Societee!
ALL: Arms high, skirts lifted so, etc.
DANCE.
Currie and Indru exit dancing, each taking two girls. Punka follows last.
Enter Pyjama in Rajah's robes, with attendants.
PYJAMA (*seeing Punka*): Stop, fellow!
PUNKA: Oh, I was looking for you I wanted to show you
PYJAMA: What is it?
PUNKA (*handing up scroll*): Read!

PYJAMA: What's this? (*Collapses*)

PUNKA: Too bad of Bumbo, isn't it? (*Chuckles*) I haven't told the others yet. I thought I'd bring you the good news first. Don't give up, old chap! Be brave! Think what a nice family party we shall make, and what fun there'll be.

PYJAMA: Fun? There will be no fun.

PUNKA: Oh, yes, there will for the crocodiles.

PYJAMA: Don't!

PUNKA: I've arranged for a photographer to take us in a family group before we are pitched into the water, and no expense will be spared to make the function a huge success.

PYJAMA: Stay! I am not your cousin!

PUNKA: What?

PYJAMA: I merely claimed a relationship to obtain a post at Court.

PUNKA: Good Heavens! And the others?

PYJAMA: Just the same they're not your cousins, either.

PUNKA (*upset*): Then I suppose you'll none of you be included in the execution?

PYJAMA: No; but we'll all come and look on. You'd better get ready.

PUNKA: Oh, I'm in no great hurry. I'll tell them to discharge the orchestra. (*Going*)

PYJAMA: No such thing. Bumbo decreed that you should die in half an hour; there's only ten minutes left. Await me at the Palace gates. (*To Punka*) There'll be lots of fun for the crocodiles, eh?

PUNKA (*aside*): I don't think so much of that joke, after all.

Exit Punka.

Enter at back Currie, looking anxiously about.

CURRIE: Where's Punka got to? (*Sees Pyjama*) Your Ex I mean, your Highness. (*Salaams*)

PYJAMA: What, Currie back again! The proprietor of the cleverest Nautch troupe in Hindustan.

CURRIE (*with ineffable conceit*): Your Highness the only Nautch troupe in the world.

PYJAMA: Haven't I always said so? (*Beebee, Banyan, Kalee, and Tiffin enter quietly at back, and listen*) Wasn't I always one of your best patrons?

CURRIE: Ye yes. (*Aside*) He always came with an order.

PYJAMA (*seeing Beebee*): What, Beebee too! Fascinating little Beebee! This is splendid. (*Rubbing his hands*) We'll have such an entertainment in the grounds this evening. Under the immediate patronage of His Highness Pyjama, Rajah of Chutneypore my name in large capitals, you know.

CURRIE: How can I express

PYJAMA: Don't! There is nothing I adore so much as one of those vocal dances of yours. (*To Beebee*) Oh, you little Terpsichorean chick-a-biddy!

BEEBEE (*aside to Currie*): A last chance! We might keep Pyjama here and make him miss the hour of the execution. That headstrong Idol may then turn his anger against Pyjama and forget his prey.

BANYAN (*to Pyjama*): You haven't seen me dance!

KALEE: You haven't heard me sing!

TIFFIN: I've improved wonderfully since I've been away.

ALL THREE: Like to see our notices? (*Producing simultaneously newspaper cuttings*)

PYJAMA: Their notices! The darlings!

BEEBEE (*coming down and roguishly confronting him*): Would you like to hear my latest song and dance?

PYJAMA: Dee-licious idea! (*To Currie*) Let them begin at once!

CURRIE: Certainly, your Majesty! Girls, take your places!

During Symphony Currie places seat for pyjama, gives him programme, refuses, scandalized, to take a fee, and hands him opera-glasses. Courtiers and Poor Relations enter.

VOCAL NAUTCH DANCE.
BEEBEE, CURRIE, BANYAN, KALEE, TIFFIN, CHORUS.

BEEBEE: Gently bear my lady to her chamber,
OTHERS: Cubbadar, Cubbadar, Cubbadar!
BEEBEE: Lay her softly on her silken bed;
OTHERS: Cubbadar, Cubbadar, Cubbadar!
BEEBEE: Lightly spread her tresses o'er the pillow,
OTHERS: Cubbadar, Cubbadar, Cubbadar!
BEEBEE: Draw the curtains close about her head.
OTHERS: Cubbadar, Cubbadar, Cubbadar!
BEEBEE: Quickly close the window o'er the river,
OTHERS: Cubbadar, Cubbadar, Cubbadar!
BEEBEE: Lock the door, and quench the flaring light,
OTHERS: Cubbadar, Cubbadar, Cubbadar!

MEN: Uzz!
BEEBEE: Buzzing comes the plundering mosquito,
OTHERS: Cubbadar, Cubbadar, Cubbadar!
MEN: Uzz!
BEEBEE: Like a brawling bandit of the night.
OTHERS: Cubbadar, Cubbadar, Cubbadar!
ALL: Uzz.

ENSEMBLE.

BEEBEE.	OTHERS.
Hark! he comes!	Uzz! etc.
How he hums!	

Nearer, nearer he approaches,
 Through the darkness, like an Evil One;
Closer, closer he encroaches;
 Whisper! he is pausing! Hush! Hush!
OTHERS: Uzz!
BEEBEE: He's gone!
The others give a buzzing accompaniment in imitation of a mosquito.
BEEBEE: Tenderly allay my lady's terror,
OTHERS: Cubbadar, Cubbadar, Cubbadar!
BEEBEE: Close her eyes and bid her sink to rest.
OTHERS: Cubbadar, Cubbadar, Cubbadar!
BEEBEE: Gently rock her into peaceful slumber,
OTHERS: Cubbadar, Cubbadar, Cubbadar!
BEEBEE: Chant the lullaby she loves the best.
OTHERS: Cubbadar, Cubbadar, Cubbadar!
BEEBEE: Silent now is all the sleeping city,
OTHERS: Cubbadar, Cubbadar, Cubbadar!
BEEBEE: Save the splash upon the distant shore.
OTHERS: Cubbadar, Cubbadar, Cubbadar!
MEN: Uzz!
BEEBEE: Listen! Once again comes the mosquito!
OTHERS: Cubbadar, Cubbadar, Cubbadar!
MEN: Uzz!
BEEBEE: Buzzing at my lady's chamber door.
OTHERS: Cubbadar, Cubbadar, Cubbadar!
ALL: Uzz!

BEEBEE: Hark! he comes, etc.

After dance, thunder and lightning. Enter Bumbo, with Chinna on his arm, followed by Attendants. Currie and the Girls go up.

BUMBO: I am disappointed in you, Pyjama! For twenty minutes I have been waiting the arrival of that pleasant tickling sensation, and I have waited in vain. (*Sternly*) Produce the prisoners!

Punka and Indru enter in charge of guards.

PUNKA: One moment excuse me I have an important communication to make. (*Advancing to Bumbo, pointing to his eye, and speaking with great warmth*) Behind that green shade is a cavity.

BUMBO (*furious and threatening*): Ah!

PUNKA: In that cavity there once reposed a diamond. (*Bumbo, enraged, lifts his hand*) That diamond was one dark night extracted. (*Bumbo buries his face in his hands*) The thief was Pyjama!
Bumbo, speechless, turns to Pyjama, who trembles and collapses as Bumbo strides towards him. Bumbo motions Priests, who seize Pyjama and take him off.

PUNKA (*aside*): At last! It's a joke that has no turning!

BUMBO: Away with them!

CHINNA (*appealing to Bumbo*): Spare them for my sake!

BEEBEE: And for mine! (*She and Chinna get one on each side of him. Bumbo is obviously amenable to the charms of female beauty, and turning to Beebee*)

BUMBO: What a pretty face! (*Chucks her chin; annoyance of Chinna, who pulls him away*) Very sorry, but I could not disappoint the dear crocodiles. (*Violently*) Take them away! (*Playfully to Beebee*) Bye, bye! (*Starts, with his eye riveted on the pendant at her neck*) Ha!

CHINNA: What is the matter, dear?

BUMBO: It is my left eye! Do you see?

CHINNA: Where?

BUMBO: My left eye suspended round that sweet creature's neck! Come to my arms. my long lost eye! (*Embraces Beebee; Chinna pulls him away; turning to Beebee again*) But how did you come by that jewel?

BEEBEE: It was left at the stage door.

BUMBO: Anonymous, I presume?

BEEBEE (*indignant*): Anonymous, of course. I should not have received it otherwise. (*Generous incredulity*) But he called the next day. (*General relief*)

INDRU (*angrily, stepping forward*): Ah!

BEEBEE: Then I told him I could not love him, and he must take the diamond back; but he wouldn't, and said I must keep it, and it would bring me luck.

BUMBO: And so it shall! You have, my girl, removed my greatest sorrow, and in return I will grant you any request you like to make.

BEEBEE: Let Punka and Indru be acquitted and restored to their rank!

BUMBO: Hum! Well, I suppose I must. (*Punka is released, Indru comes forward and throws off his disguise*)

PUNKA: My dear Bumbo, you're a brick! (*Slapping him on back*)

BUMBO: I'm not a brick, I'm a wooden idol, and if you strike me on the back again, I shall retaliate in a manner that you will not enjoy. (*Addressing the diamond*) You beauty! (*Kisses it*) I thought I should never see you or see with you again! Bless you! (*To those near him*) Pardon me! (*Removes the shade from his eye, appears to press the diamond into its place, and then looks about with eyes wide open*) How's that?

PUNKA: Not out!

INDRU: Charming!

PUNKA: Suits you admirably!

BUMBO: Yes, I think it does. Upon my word, it makes me feel fifteen hundred years younger. (*Struts. Then to Chinna*) You are still willing to be an Idol's bride?

CHINNA (*nodding*): Anybody's bride will do.

BUMBO: And to be turned into wood, and sit always by my side? (*Chinna assents*) Fetch the throne. Bless you, my children! And now for a roar of cannons, a crash of bells, and a blare of trumpets, and Bumbo will return to his shelf for ever!

FINALE OF ACT II.

BUMBO: And this is the Idol, grave and staid,
CHINNA: That wooed and won the simple maid,
BANYAN: That came to be of Punka's train
TIFFIN: By means of the ingenious brain
INDRU: Which sent my Beebee o'er the main
BEEBEE: To where I practised once again
CURRIE: The dainty step her teacher taught,
  Which from her fond admirer bought
KALEE: The wondrous, rare, and precious stone

BUMBO: That saved my eyesight,

PUNKA: And the throne
    Of the Rajah of Chutneypore;

ALL: Of the Rajah of Chutneypore!

INDRU: For long may my father in happiness reign.

ALL: Vive, vive, sa Majesté!

CHINNA: And long may my Bumbo my Idol remain!

ALL: Vive, vive, sa Majesté!

BEEBEE (*to Indru*): And ne'er may your heart from your Beebee
    remove,

ALL: Vive, vive, sa Majesté!

PUNKA: And long may the public my edicts approve.

ALL: Vive, vive, sa Majesté!
        Vive, vive tout ce qu'arrive,
    Vive, vive, sa Majesté!

Sedan chair brought on. Bumbo and Chinna take their places in it, and make angular and eccentric motions indicative of turning to wood. The Priests take them up, and are carrying them off to the temple at the descent of the

CURTAIN

A Note About the Author

George Dance (1857–1932) and Frank Desprez (1853–1916) were both prominent contributors to nineteenth-century theater. The England-born talents held different roles including journalists and editors but thrived as playwrights. Some of Dance's work includes *Ma mie Rosette*, *The Gay Parisienne* and *A Chinese Honeymoon*, while Desprez wrote *La fille de Madame Angot*, *A Private Wire* and *Quite an Adventure*. In 1891, they would eventually collaborate on the successful comic opera, *The Rajah of Chutneypore*.

A Note from the Publisher

Spanning many genres, from non-fiction essays to literature classics to children's books and lyric poetry, Mint Edition books showcase the master works of our time in a modern new package. The text is freshly typeset, is clean and easy to read, and features a new note about the author in each volume. Many books also include exclusive new introductory material. Every book boasts a striking new cover, which makes it as appropriate for collecting as it is for gift giving. Mint Edition books are only printed when a reader orders them, so natural resources are not wasted. We're proud that our books are never manufactured in excess and exist only in the exact quantity they need to be read and enjoyed.

bookfinity™

Discover more of your favorite classics with Bookfinity™.

- Track your reading with custom book lists.
- Get great book recommendations for your personalized Reader Type.
- Add reviews for your favorite books.
- AND MUCH MORE!

Visit **bookfinity.com** and take the fun Reader Type quiz to get started.

Enjoy our classic and modern companion pairings!

Classic & Modern